CW01651106

Verbal Activity

CEM Style 20 Minute Tests 21-40

TESTBOOK 2

Dr Stephen C Curran
with Katrina MacKay
Edited by Andrea Richardson
Illustrated by Natalie Knowles

This book belongs to

Accelerated Education Publications Ltd.

Verbal Activity Test 21

Read the following passage carefully.

The USA joined the First World War in 1917 and Corporal Robert Conroy of the 102nd Infantry had to go and fight. While training with his regiment in Connecticut he found a Bull Terrier wandering the grounds. He adopted the dog and named him Stubby because of his short tail. Stubby was fairly small with a brown and white coat. He was an alert, polite and excitable dog, who took to training well.

Conroy hid Stubby on the ship to France and, upon arrival, he concealed him under his overcoat. When Conroy's commanding officer discovered him, Stubby saluted him as he had been trained to in camp, and the commanding officer allowed the dog to stay on the Western Front. Stubby served for 18 months and participated in seventeen battles.

He warned his regiment of surprise mustard gas attacks, as he could hear the drone of incoming artillery shells before humans could. He also located wounded soldiers in no-man's-land and comforted those in pain. He was injured during a gas attack and also wounded in the foreleg by a hand grenade. Stubby was sent to the rear for convalescence and, as he had done on the front, he improved morale. After recovery he returned with a specially designed gas mask to protect him. Stubby once caught a German spy by grabbing his trousers, holding him there until American soldiers found him. The commander of the 102nd Infantry nominated Stubby for the rank of sergeant. He was the only dog ever to receive this promotion. Sergeant Stubby had a chamois coat on which his medals were pinned.

At the end of the war Robert Conroy smuggled Sergeant Stubby home. The dog died in his sleep in 1926.

<u>Notes on Text:</u>
First World War – 1914-1918
Chamois (line 21) – a type of soft leather

Now answer the following questions.

1) For how many years did Robert Conroy care for Sergeant Stubby?

- [ ] a) 7 years
- [ ] b) 8 years
- [ ] c) 9 years
- [ ] d) 10 years

© 2015 Stephen Curran

2) What was Conroy doing when he found the dog?

- [ ] a) Taking part in military exercises
- [ ] b) Fighting in a battle
- [ ] c) Recovering from an injury
- [ ] d) Travelling on a ship

3) Why was Stubby allowed to stay on the Western Front?

- [ ] a) Stubby was very friendly.
- [ ] b) The commanding officer could see that the dog was well-trained.
- [ ] c) The troops enjoyed the dog's company.
- [ ] d) He helped wounded soldiers.

4) What does the word 'convalescence' (line 16) mean?

- [ ] a) The comfort of others
- [ ] b) An enjoyable holiday
- [ ] c) To change regiment
- [ ] d) Rest and recuperation

5) Why was Stubby's ability to listen so valuable in battle?

- [ ] a) He could hear the cries of wounded soldiers.
- [ ] b) He could hear things that the soldiers failed to detect.
- [ ] c) He could hear soldiers attacking.
- [ ] d) He was not startled by the sound of bombs exploding.

6) How was Stubby rewarded for his actions in the war?

- [ ] a) He was made a sergeant.
- [ ] b) He was provided with special food.
- [ ] c) He was given a chamois coat.
- [ ] d) He was permitted to go home with Conroy after the war.

7) What was Stubby given to help defend himself?

- [ ] a) A bulletproof vest
- [ ] b) A chamois coat
- [ ] c) A special respirator
- [ ] d) A dog helmet

8) Why is Stubby a good example of how dogs relate to human beings?

- [ ] a) He encouraged the soldiers to take exercise.
- [ ] b) He protected the soldiers against every aggressor.
- [ ] c) He amused the soldiers with funny tricks.
- [ ] d) He provided solace and companionship.

9) For how long did Stubby participate in World War One?

- [ ] a) One and a half years
- [ ] b) Seventeen months
- [ ] c) One year
- [ ] d) 102 days

10) How did Stubby's physical attributes benefit him?

- [ ] a) The colour of his fur was good camouflage.
- [ ] b) His size meant that he could be easily kept out of sight.
- [ ] c) His tail did not get caught in equipment.
- [ ] d) His weight meant that he could pin down intruders.

Choose the word that has a similar meaning to the words in both sets of brackets.

11) (decorate, adorn) (floor, platform) — deck ground embellish stage trim

12) (peal, strike) (charge, fee) — clang tariff hit cost toll

13) (leap, bound) (origin, source) — jump spring cause font hurdle

14) (stake, post) (wan, ashen) — pole grey pasty pale stick

15) (disorder, disarray) (quandary, problem) — chaos dilemma mess predicament jam

© 2015 Stephen Curran

Complete the word on the right so that it means the same as, or nearly the same as, the word on the left.

16) **worldwide**

	n		v	e		s	a	

17) **nice**

p		e		s		n	t

18) **toxic**

p			s		n	o		s

19) **insulting**

o	f		e		s		v	

20) **famous**

r	e			w		e	d

Choose the word that means the opposite of the word on the left.

21) **flounder**	flail ☐	prosper ☐	hesitate ☐	shelve ☐
22) **absurd**	foolish ☐	sensible ☐	farcical ☐	crazy ☐
23) **magical**	enchanted ☐	special ☐	mundane ☐	mystic ☐
24) **lethargy**	stupor ☐	allergy ☐	deadly ☐	energy ☐
25) **old**	archaic ☐	current ☐	mature ☐	newsworthy ☐

Score ☐ **Percentage**

© 2015 Stephen Curran

Verbal Activity Test 22

Read the following passage carefully.

The Captain's Daughter

We were crowded in the cabin,
Not a soul would dare to sleep,
It was midnight on the waters,
And a storm was on the deep.

"Tis a fearful thing in winter
To be shattered by the blast,
And to hear the rattling trumpet
Thunder, "Cut away the mast!"

So we shuddered there in silence,
For the stoutest held his breath,
While the hungry sea was roaring
And the breakers talked with Death.

As thus we sat in darkness,
Each one busy with his prayers,
"We are lost!" the captain shouted
As he staggered down the stairs.

But his little daughter whispered,
As she took his icy hand,
"Isn't God, upon the ocean,
Just the same as on the land?"

Then we kissed the little maiden.
And we spoke in better cheer,
And we anchored safe in harbour
When the morn was shining clear.

By James T Fields (1817-1881).

Now answer the following questions.

1) What is the rhyming pattern of each stanza in this poem?

- [ ] a) ABCB
- [ ] b) ABAB
- [ ] c) ABAC
- [ ] d) ABBA

© 2015 Stephen Curran

2) What important reassurance did the daughter give to the sailors?

- [ ] a) She said the storm would pass.
- [ ] b) She had prayed to God.
- [ ] c) She held people's hands.
- [ ] d) God would save them.

3) What sort of poetry is this?

- [ ] a) Sonnet
- [ ] b) Lyric
- [ ] c) Narrative
- [ ] d) Epic

4) What does 'For the stoutest held his breath' (line 10) mean?

- [ ] a) They were exhausted from trying to save the ship.
- [ ] b) Even the bravest sailors were scared.
- [ ] c) They were about to go underwater.
- [ ] d) They were saving their energy.

5) How many stressed beats are there in each line?

- [ ] a) Four
- [ ] b) Five
- [ ] c) Seven
- [ ] d) Eight

6) What did the sailors fear might happen to their ship?

- [ ] a) It would founder on the rocks.
- [ ] b) The storm would demast it.
- [ ] c) The sails would be lost.
- [ ] d) It would break the rudder.

7) Which poetic technique is used in line 12?

- [ ] a) Personification
- [ ] b) Anaphora
- [ ] c) Simile
- [ ] d) Assonance

8) When did the storm occur?

- [ ] a) On a frosty winter morning
- [ ] b) In summer at noon
- [ ] c) On a winters night
- [ ] d) At dusk in autumn

9) Which two poetic techniques are used in line 11?

- [ ] a) Personification and simile
- [ ] b) Metaphor and personification
- [ ] c) Hyperbole and alliteration
- [ ] d) Consonance and metaphor

10) What is the theme or message of this poem?

- [ ] a) Nature
- [ ] b) Wisdom
- [ ] c) Suffering
- [ ] d) Hope

Select the correct words to complete the passage.

The clarinet is an instrument of the **11)** [ ] woodwind / [ ] woodwork / [ ] woodland family. It is a single **12)** [ ] read / [ ] reed / [ ] raid instrument that is played by **13)** [ ] blowing / [ ] reading / [ ] pressing into a mouthpiece. The term clarinet comes from the French word 'clarion', which **14)** [ ] defines / [ ] similar / [ ] means 'little trumpet'. First **15)** [ ] discovered / [ ] invented / [ ] thought by Johann Denner in seventeenth **16)** [ ] century / [ ] year / [ ] decade Germany, the clarinet is a **17)** [ ] descendant / [ ] ancestor / [ ] formed of the French

© 2015 Stephen Curran

instrument chalumeau, which included eight **18)** ☐ thumb ☐ toe ☐ finger holes at the front and one at the back for the thumb. The modern clarinet is **19)** ☐ played ☐ pressed ☐ plaid by placing pads over the holes as well as the fingers. It was the last instrument to be included in a symphony **20)** ☐ group ☐ orchestra ☐ choir .

Complete the word on the right so that it means the opposite of the word on the left.

21) **present**

	b		e		t

22) **endanger**

p		o	t			t

23) **inventive**

u		i		a	g		n		t	i		e

24) **supportive**

u	n		e			f	u	

25) **thoughtless**

	o	n		i	d		r		t	e

Score ☐ Percentage

© 2015 Stephen Curran

Verbal Activity Test 23

Read the following passage carefully.

A lion lay asleep in the forest, his great head resting on his paws. A plucky mouse came upon him unexpectedly. The mouse admired the lion's ears, his long whiskers and his great mane.

"Since he's sleeping," said the mouse, "he'll never suspect I'm here!" With that, the mouse climbed onto the lion's tail. She ran across his back and even his face, then slid down a leg and jumped off of the paw. The lion awoke, was irritated and caught the mouse between his claws.

He was about to kill it when the mouse begged, "Please, spare me! Let me go and I'll surely repay you someday for your kindness."

The idea that such an insignificant creature was able to do anything for him made the lion laugh so much that he had to hold his belly.

"You are so small! How could you ever help me?" The lion let the mouse go. She jumped to her freedom and ran away.

The next day, hunters came to the jungle and set a huge rope snare in the lion's lair. When the lion returned from hunting, he stepped into the trap. He roared and wept, but could not free himself. The mouse heard the lion's pitiful roar and ran back to help him. She found the one thick rope that held it together and gnawed and nibbled until the rope snapped. The lion shook off the remaining ropes and broke free.

"There!" said the mouse, "you laughed at me when I promised to repay you: but now you see it is possible for even a mouse to help a lion."

The lion replied, "Dear friend, I was foolish to ridicule you for being so small. You helped save my life."

'The Lion and the Mouse' adapted from *Aesop's Fables*.

Now answer the following questions.

1) What is the moral of this tale?

- [ ] a) Lions and mice can be friends.
- [ ] b) A kindness is never wasted.
- [ ] c) Hunting lions is cruel.
- [ ] d) Size is important.

© 2015 Stephen Curran

2) How did the hunters restrain the lion?

- [ ] a) They bound him.
- [ ] b) They kept him in a pit.
- [ ] c) He was watched at gunpoint.
- [ ] d) They sedated him.

3) What humoured the lion?

- [ ] a) The size of the mouse.
- [ ] b) That the mouse had got so close to him while asleep.
- [ ] c) That the mouse begged for its life.
- [ ] d) The idea a mouse could assist him in any way.

4) Which word do you think best describes the mouse's character?

- [ ] a) Timid
- [ ] b) Grouchy
- [ ] c) Bold
- [ ] d) Passive

5) How did the mouse free the lion?

- [ ] a) She chewed through the fibres.
- [ ] b) She untied the lion.
- [ ] c) She woke up the lion who broke free.
- [ ] d) She got other mice to help her chew through the rope.

6) Which two adjectives best describe the change in the lion's attitude towards the mouse?

- [ ] a) From loathing to thankful
- [ ] b) From scornful to arrogant
- [ ] c) From mocking to grateful
- [ ] d) From intrigued to admiring

7) Which best describes the progress of the mouse along the lion's body?

- [ ] a) Tail, back, leg, face, paw
- [ ] b) Paw, leg, face, back, tail
- [ ] c) Tail, face, back, leg, paw
- [ ] d) Tail, back, face, leg, paw

ae © 2015 Stephen Curran

8) Why did the mouse feel so confident she would not be detected?

- [ ] a) The lion was slumbering.
- [ ] b) She was small and light.
- [ ] c) She would be quick.
- [ ] d) The lion would not mind.

9) What did the mouse think of the lion at the start of the story?

- [ ] a) She disliked the lion because he hunted smaller animals.
- [ ] b) She appreciated his physique.
- [ ] c) She disapproved of him because he laughed at her.
- [ ] d) She was fearful of his size and strength.

10) How did the mouse persuade the lion to free her?

- [ ] a) She agreed to free the lion from the hunters.
- [ ] b) She rebuked the lion for being a bully.
- [ ] c) She promised to do the lion a favour.
- [ ] d) She told the lion that other animals would avenge her.

Choose the word that means the same as the word on the left.

11) **badger**	fox	pester	fester	pest
12) **earnest**	sincere	frivolous	listened	secret
13) **vivacious**	dull	loud	abrupt	lively
14) **qualified**	charred	character	chartered	charitable
15) **crucial**	vital	slight	painful	trivial

© 2015 Stephen Curran

Four of the words in each list are linked. Mark the rectangle under the word that is NOT related to these four.

16)	blasé	nonchalant	tense	jaded	carefree
	☐	☐	☐	☐	☐
17)	hardware	pear	nightmare	prayer	appear
	☐	☐	☐	☐	☐
18)	ladybird	beetle	ant	dragonfly	wasp
	☐	☐	☐	☐	☐
19)	sully	taint	filter	soil	pollute
	☐	☐	☐	☐	☐
20)	dishonour	disgrace	discredit	disrepute	degradation
	☐	☐	☐	☐	☐

Complete the word on the right so that it means the opposite of the word on the left.

21) **brave**

c	o		a			l	

22) **adequate**

	n	s		f		i	c			n	t

23) **omit**

i		c			d	

24) **boisterous**

	l		c		d

25) **focused**

i	n		t		e	n		i	v	

Score ☐ **Percentage**  %

Verbal Activity Test 24

Read the following passage carefully.

Wright Flyer Soars Three Miles in High Wind

Success after Three Years of Hard Work by Ohio Brothers

ACCOMPLISHED WHAT LANGLEY FAILED AT

Huge Machine Flies, with Man as Passenger, under Perfect Control

The problem of aerial navigation without the use of a balloon has finally been solved.

Over the North Carolina coast yesterday, near Kitty Hawk, two Ohio inventors proved that they could soar through the air in a flying machine of their own construction, costing only $1,000. They could steer and speed it at will. It flew at roughly 7mph in headwinds of up to 27mph.

Like a monster bird, the invention hovered above the breakers and circled over the rolling sand hills. Commanded by its navigator it flew for three miles, then gracefully descended to earth and rested lightly upon the spot selected by the pilot.

The United States government has spent over $50,000 to date funding the ideas of the astronomer and inventor Professor Samuel Pierpont Langley (1834-) of the Smithsonian Institute. So far, he has successfully created an unmanned powered

aircraft that was launched from a catapult and flew over 1,000 metres at 25mph and crash-landed.

Meanwhile, Wilbur and Orville Wright, two brothers in their thirties, have been secretly perfecting their invention based on their observations of bird flight and have successfully tested it. They are not yet ready for the world to know their methods in conquering the air, but the Virginian-Pilot newspaper can officially state the dimensions of their invention.

The box kite timber framework is 33 feet wide, five feet deep and five feet long and covered with tough canvas. A gasoline engine is suspended centrally below. It has two six-bladed propellers and a fan-shaped canvas steering-gear to control it.

An adapted extract from *The Virginian-Pilot*, Norfolk, USA, 18th December 1903.

Notes on Text:

mph (line 11) – miles per hour
1,000 metres (line 29) – roughly two thirds of a mile

© 2015 Stephen Curran

Now answer the following questions.

1) How much faster, under test conditions, was Langley's plane than the Wright brothers'?

- [ ] a) 2mph
- [ ] b) 6mph
- [ ] c) 18mph
- [ ] d) 20mph

2) What was the main difference between the *Wright Flyer* and Langley's plane?

- [ ] a) Langley's plane had a larger wingspan and flew much further.
- [ ] b) The Wright brothers' plane was piloted.
- [ ] c) Langley's plane did not have an engine.
- [ ] d) The Wright brothers' plane had propellers.

3) Who built the *Wright Flyer*?

- [ ] a) The US Government
- [ ] b) Professor Langley
- [ ] c) The Smithsonian Institute
- [ ] d) Wilbur and Orville Wright

4) How did the Wright brothers guide their plane?

- [ ] a) With a rudder
- [ ] b) With the propellers
- [ ] c) By weight distribution
- [ ] d) With an electronic navigation device

5) Which form of transportation did powered flight replace?

- [ ] a) Hot air balloon
- [ ] b) Flight by catapult
- [ ] c) Zeppelin
- [ ] d) Horse-drawn transport

6) What were the main materials used to construct the *Wright Flyer*?

- [ ] a) Steel and fabric
- [ ] b) Wood and cloth
- [ ] c) Plastic and canvas
- [ ] d) Timber and papier mâché

ae © 2015 Stephen Curran

7) What did the Wright brother's achievement demonstrate?

☐ a) Investing huge amounts of money in invention pays off.
☐ b) Creative ideas matter less than education and expertise.
☐ c) Inspiration is more important than funding.
☐ d) Age and experience matter more than youthful enthusiasm.

8) Where did the Wright brothers perform their test flight?

☐ a) On the Norfolk coastline
☐ b) At the Smithsonian Institute
☐ c) On the North Carolina runway
☐ d) On a beach near Kitty Hawk

9) What fuel did the *Wright Flyer* require?

☐ a) Gas
☐ b) Petrol
☐ c) Timber
☐ d) Wind

10) What was most significant about the end of the Wright brother's flight?

☐ a) The plane crashed.
☐ b) The plane landed successfully.
☐ c) The plane landed at a precise location.
☐ d) The plane landed undamaged.

Fill in the missing letters to complete the passage.

A farmer was **11)** [s][ ][w][i][ ][g] seeds. These seeds fell in many

12) [d][ ][f][ ][e][r][ ][n][ ] places: a path, a rocky area with shallow soil,

13) [t][ ][o][r][ ][y] shrubbery and good soil. Birds flew down and ate all of

the seeds that fell on the path. Where the seeds fell onto a rocky area, the plants

14) [s][ ][r][ ][n][g] up quickly. However, they were soon

15) [b][ ][r][ ][ ] in the sun because they had been **16)** [u][ ][a][ ][l][ ]

© 2015 Stephen Curran

to grow roots in the **17)** [s][ ][a][ ][l][ ][w] soil. Those that fell onto the shrubbery grew, but were soon **18)** [c][ ][o][ ][e][ ] by the thorns. Lastly, the seeds that fell on good soil grew to **19)** [ ][r][o][ ][u][ ][e] a good **20)** [y][ ][ ][l][d].

Rearrange the words so that each sentence makes sense. Underline the word which does NOT fit into the sentence.

21) to please I yours toilet go the may

22) the storey sentence words can in this reshuffle

23) have to complete you tests your five forty minutes has

24) chose your first characters scenario the choose and

25) friend puppies birthday a best her for wants puppy my

Score [ ] **Percentage** [%]

ae © 2015 Stephen Curran

Verbal Activity Test 25

Read the following passage carefully.

The Owl and the Pussy-Cat

The Owl and the Pussy-cat went to sea
In a beautiful pea green boat,
They took some honey, and plenty of money,
Wrapped up in a five pound note.
The Owl looked up to the stars above,
And sang to a small guitar,
'O lovely Pussy! O Pussy my love,
What a beautiful Pussy you are,
You are,
You are!
What a beautiful Pussy you are!'

Pussy said to the Owl, 'You elegant fowl!
How charmingly sweet you sing!
O let us be married! too long we have tarried:
But what shall we do for a ring?'
They sailed away, for a year and a day,
To the land where the Bong-tree grows
And there in a wood a Piggy-wig stood
With a ring at the end of his nose,
His nose,
His nose,
With a ring at the end of his nose.

'Dear pig, are you willing to sell for one shilling
Your ring?' Said the Piggy, 'I will.'
So they took it away, and were married next day
By the Turkey who lives on the hill.
They dined on mince, and slices of quince,
Which they ate with a runcible spoon;
And hand in hand, on the edge of the sand,
They danced by the light of the moon,
The moon,
The moon,
They danced by the light of the moon.

By Edward Lear (1812-1888)

© 2015 Stephen Curran

Notes on Text:

One shilling (line 23) – old-fashioned English money. There used to be twenty shillings to a pound.

Quince (line 27) – a type of fruit

Runcible spoon (line 28) – Lear's invented word is now used to describe a spork (a combination of spoon and fork)

Now answer the following questions.

1) How did the pig assist the couple?
- [ ] a) He sold them the ring from his nose.
- [ ] b) He steered their boat.
- [ ] c) He performed their wedding ceremony.
- [ ] d) He sang them a song with the turkey.

2) Which lines in each stanza always rhyme?
- [ ] a) The 1st and 3rd
- [ ] b) The 2nd and 4th
- [ ] c) The 4th and 5th
- [ ] d) The 5th and 7th

3) Which poetic technique is used at the end of every stanza?
- [ ] a) Onomatopoeia
- [ ] b) Metaphor
- [ ] c) Anaphora
- [ ] d) Hyperbole

4) What did the owl and the pussycat take with them on their journey?
- [ ] a) Honey, money and a guitar
- [ ] b) Mince and quince
- [ ] c) Honey, money and a ring
- [ ] d) Mince, quince and a runcible spoon

5) What type of poetry is this poem?
- [ ] a) Nonsense
- [ ] b) Sonnet
- [ ] c) Limerick
- [ ] d) Epic

ae © 2015 Stephen Curran

6) What does the word 'tarried' (line 14) mean?

- [ ] a) Hurried
- [ ] b) Lived
- [ ] c) Journeyed
- [ ] d) Waited

7) Where did the couple dance?

- [ ] a) On the shoreline
- [ ] b) In the forest
- [ ] c) On the hill
- [ ] d) In their boat

8) On which day of their voyage did the couple marry?

- [ ] a) Day 364
- [ ] b) Day 365
- [ ] c) Day 366
- [ ] d) Day 367

9) What did the owl pay for the ring?

- [ ] a) A five pound note
- [ ] b) A shilling
- [ ] c) Some honey
- [ ] d) A pound

10) What is the mood of the poem?

- [ ] a) Ecstatic
- [ ] b) Peaceful
- [ ] c) Humorous
- [ ] d) Pessimistic

Complete the word on the right so that it means the same as, or nearly the same as, the word on the left.

11) **woeful** | m | | s | | r | | b | | e |

12) **calm** | t | r | | n | | u | i | |

13) **discard** | | b | a | | d | | n |

© 2015 Stephen Curran ae

14)	**amusing**		n	t	e		t	a			i	n	
15)	**damage**	v	a		d		l		s				

Choose the word that has a similar meaning to the words in both sets of brackets.

16) (book, publication)
(capacity, size)
tome bulk volume mass paperback

17) (position, grade)
(offensive, nasty)
rank stance foul rude status

18) (bring, buy)
(meaning, substance)
carry purchase core import sense

19) (stick, catch)
(preserve, marmalade)
grasp jam conserve gum jelly

20) (boulder, stone)
(oscillate, sway)
shingle waver grit swing rock

Choose the word that means the opposite of the word on the left.

21) **discard**	keep ☐	shed ☐	conceal ☐	abandon ☐
22) **break**	chance ☐	rupture ☐	mend ☐	vacation ☐
23) **grand**	major ☐	striking ☐	distinguished ☐	ordinary ☐
24) **abundant**	scarce ☐	plentiful ☐	violent ☐	ample ☐
25) **anxious**	eager ☐	calm ☐	nervous ☐	average ☐

Score ☐ **Percentage**

© 2015 Stephen Curran

Verbal Activity Test 26

Read the following passage carefully.

Oliver Twist has left his home and travelled to London. He collapses from exhaustion in a shop doorway. A young boy crosses over to him:

"Hullo, my covey!"

The boy was about Oliver's age, but the oddest looking he had ever seen. He was a dirty, snub-nosed boy who had the airs and manners of a man. He was short for his age with bow-legs and little, sharp, ugly eyes. His hat was stuck on his head so lightly, that it threatened to fall off at every moment—and would have done so if he had not had a knack of giving his head a sudden twitch, which brought it back to its old place again. He wore a man's coat, which reached his heels. He had turned the cuffs back, half-way up his arm, to get his hands out of the sleeves.

"I am very hungry and tired," said Oliver tearfully, "I've been walking seven days."

"Sivin days!" replied the young gentleman. "Going to London?"

"Yes."

"Any lodgings?"

"No."

"Money?"

"No."

The boy whistled and put his arms into his pockets.

"Do you live in London?" inquired Oliver.

"I do," replied the boy. "I suppose you want some place to sleep tonight?"

"Yes," answered Oliver. "I've not slept under a roof since I left."

"Don't fret your eyelids," said the young gentleman. "I've got to be in London tonight; and I know a 'spectable old gentleman called Fagin as lives there, wot'll give you lodgings for nothink, and never ask for change."

This offer of shelter was too tempting to be resisted and Oliver vowed to make a good impression on Fagin. In conversation Oliver discovered that his friend's name was Jack Dawkins, and was nicknamed 'The Artful Dodger'.

An adapted extract from *Oliver Twist* by Charles Dickens (1812-1870).

© 2015 Stephen Curran

Now answer the following questions.

1) How did Jack keep his hat on his head?

☐ a) He used a hatpin.
☐ b) He jolted his head.
☐ c) He held it with his hand.
☐ d) He stuck it on his head with tape.

2) What did Oliver have with him?

☐ a) A man's coat
☐ b) Some coins
☐ c) Some food
☐ d) Only his clothes

3) What accommodation did Jack suggest to Oliver?

☐ a) The Artful Dodger's hideout
☐ b) The roof Oliver had slept under
☐ c) Fagin's house
☐ d) A workhouse in London

4) What style of speech does the author use to portray Jack's level of education?

☐ a) Informal speech
☐ b) Educated speech
☐ c) A speech impediment
☐ d) Foreign speech

5) What condition was Oliver in?

☐ a) Starving and spirited
☐ b) Enthusiastic but hungry
☐ c) Weary and famished
☐ d) Exhausted but well fed

6) How much was Oliver required to pay for his upcoming night's rest?

☐ a) Nothing at all
☐ b) Seven day's labour
☐ c) The change in his pocket
☐ d) A vow to serve The Artful Dodger

ae © 2015 Stephen Curran

7) What was most unusual about Jack?

- ☐ a) He was dirty.
- ☐ b) He had a nickname.
- ☐ c) He was well dressed.
- ☐ d) He acted like an adult.

8) What does Jack's nickname imply about his personality?

- ☐ a) It suggests he was cunning and dishonest.
- ☐ b) He was clever at not blocking people's paths.
- ☐ c) It hints he was creative and artistic.
- ☐ d) He was honest and a trusty friend.

9) What was the tone of the boys' conversation?

- ☐ a) Suspicious but jovial
- ☐ b) Aggressive and coercive
- ☐ c) Confrontational but helpful
- ☐ d) Amicable and inquisitive

10) What problem did Jack's coat present for him?

- ☐ a) The coat dragged along the ground.
- ☐ b) The sleeves were too long.
- ☐ c) It draped half-way off his shoulders.
- ☐ d) The pockets were too big.

Select the correct words to complete the passage.

Spike Milligan, **11)** [☐ born / ☐ birth / ☐ birthday] on 16th April 1918 in India, is a well-known poet. His father was an Irish captain who **12)** [☐ lived / ☐ served / ☐ slept] in the British Indian Army. Inhabiting India and Burma during his **13)** [☐ adulthood / ☐ life / ☐ childhood] ,

© 2015 Stephen Curran

14) ☐ most / ☐ majority / ☐ minority of his adult life was spent in England. He **15)** ☐ followed / ☐ copies / ☐ lived his father's example and fought in the British Army **16)** ☐ during / ☐ within / ☐ through World War

II. Milligan wrote many poems, the majority of which were nonsense poems.

17) ☐ Perhaps / ☐ Sometimes / ☐ Often the most **18)** ☐ famous / ☐ infamous / ☐ favourite of these poems is *On the Ning Nang Nong*, which was voted the **19)** ☐ nation's / ☐ county's / ☐ poet's favourite in a 1998 poll of the United Kingdom. He died from liver **20)** ☐ illness / ☐ disease / ☐ sick at the age of 83.

Complete the word on the right so that it means the same as, or nearly the same as, the word on the left.

21)	**vigorous**		n	e		g	e		i	
22)	**elegant**	s	t		l		s			
23)	**downcast**	d	e		e		t	e		
24)	**shabby**	t		t			r	e		
25)	**offer**	v		l		n	t			r

Score ☐ **Percentage** ☐ %

Verbal Activity Test 27

Read the following passage carefully.

My Shadow

I have a little shadow that goes in and out with me,
And what can be the use of him is more than I can see.
He is very, very like me from the heels up to the head;
And I see him jump before me, when I jump into my bed.

The funniest thing about him is the way he likes to grow—
Not at all like proper children, which is always very slow;
For he sometimes shoots up taller like an india-rubber ball,
And he sometimes gets so little that there's none of him at all.

He hasn't got a notion of how children ought to play,
And can only make a fool of me in every sort of way.
He stays so close beside me, he's a coward you can see;
I'd think shame to stick to nursie as that shadow sticks to me!

One morning, very early, before the sun was up,
I rose and found the shining dew on every buttercup;
But my lazy little shadow, like an arrant sleepy-head,
Had stayed at home behind me and was fast asleep in bed.

By Robert Louis Stevenson (1850-1894).

Notes on Text:
nursie (line 12) – a nursemaid
arrant (line 15) – complete

Now answer the following questions.

1) What is the rhyming pattern of this poem?

- [ ] a) AABB
- [ ] b) ABCD
- [ ] c) ABBA
- [ ] d) ABAB

© 2015 Stephen Curran

2) What is the real reason why the shadow did not appear in the last stanza?

- [ ] a) The shadow was tired and lazy.
- [ ] b) The sun had not risen so it could not be seen.
- [ ] c) The shadow was asleep in bed.
- [ ] d) The sun had risen but the curtains were closed.

3) Which poetic technique is used in line 7?

- [ ] a) Metaphor
- [ ] b) Anaphora
- [ ] c) Simile
- [ ] d) Caesura

4) What is the author's opinion of the shadow in the first stanza?

- [ ] a) He thinks that it is lazy.
- [ ] b) He thinks that it is pointless.
- [ ] c) He enjoys the companionship.
- [ ] d) He think that it is foolish.

5) What is unusual about the size of the shadow?

- [ ] a) It grows in the same way as children.
- [ ] b) It is big all the time.
- [ ] c) It is always exactly the same size as the author.
- [ ] d) It keeps changing.

6) Why is the shadow considered 'a coward' (line 11)?

- [ ] a) It runs in the other direction.
- [ ] b) It sticks close to nursie.
- [ ] c) It never parts company from the author.
- [ ] d) It does not like to play on its own.

7) What is the main poetic technique used in line 12?

- [ ] a) Anaphora
- [ ] b) Simile
- [ ] c) Alliteration
- [ ] d) Hyperbole

ae © 2015 Stephen Curran

8) How would you describe the author's attitude to the shadow?

- [ ] a) Mainly playful and amusing.
- [ ] b) He sees it as a true friend.
- [ ] c) He finds it comical all the time.
- [ ] d) Mainly admiring.

9) What is the subject of this poem?

- [ ] a) Irritation at the shadow's imitation.
- [ ] b) The shadow as a companion.
- [ ] c) True friendship.
- [ ] d) The loneliness of the author.

10) What poetic technique is used in relation to the shadow throughout the poem?

- [ ] a) Hyperbole
- [ ] b) Anaphora
- [ ] c) Caricature
- [ ] d) Personification

Four of the words in each list are linked. Mark the rectangle under the word that is NOT related to these four.

11)	mood	was	paper	ward	devil
12)	idolise	vilify	worship	adore	revere
13)	Germany	Ghana	Glasgow	Guatemala	Greece
14)	introvert	introduce	intolerant	introspective	introit
15)	pay	cash	coin	change	sterling

© 2015 Stephen Curran

Rearrange the words so that each sentence makes sense. Underline the word which does NOT fit into the sentence.

16) sunny it yesterday today raining is be it supposed to but is

17) there the school zoo trip their a is to

18) ten the to read I during summer books like would films

19) ice I evening the skating weekend went at

20) today school football at to are play were taught we

Choose the word that means the opposite of the word on the left.

21) **reject**	cull ☐	assume ☐	discard ☐	accept ☐
22) **confront**	challenge ☐	avoid ☐	discomfort ☐	meet ☐
23) **remain**	leave ☐	persist ☐	forget ☐	linger ☐
24) **loose**	find ☐	secure ☐	acquire ☐	baggy ☐
25) **versatile**	adaptable ☐	loyal ☐	limited ☐	useful ☐

Score ☐ **Percentage**

ae © 2015 Stephen Curran

Verbal Activity Test 28

Read the following passage carefully.

Trot, a young girl, and Captain Bill, an ex-mariner, travel to a Magic Isle in Munchkin Country in search of a magic flower. Any living thing that makes contact with the island takes root. Dorothy and the Wizard find their friends trapped and attempt to free them.

The Wizard opened his black bag and prepared. He set up a small silver tripod and placed a gold basin on top. Into this he put two powders—one pink and one sky-blue—and poured over them a yellow liquid from a crystal vial. He mumbled some magic words, and the powders sizzled and burned. This sent a cloud of violet smoke floating across the river that enveloped Trot, Captain Bill and the toadstools on which they sat. When the smoke disappeared, the Wizard addressed the prisoners:

"Are you free?"

They tried to move their feet but failed.

"No!" they shouted.

The Wizard rubbed the top of his shiny head thoughtfully and took more magic tools from the bag.

He loaded a little black ball in a silver pistol and shot it towards the Magic Isle. It exploded just above Trot's head and scattered a thousand sparks over her.

"That should set her free," said the Wizard.

But Trot's feet were still rooted in the ground.

For an hour the Wizard worked hard, using every tool in his bag, but nothing worked.

"Dear me!" exclaimed Dorothy, "I'm afraid we'll have to go to Glinda the Good Witch, after all."

The little Wizard blushed with shame because his magic was not powerful enough.

"I won't give up yet, Dorothy," he said, "I know lots of wizardry that I haven't tried. It's like unlocking a door; all you need is to find the right key."

An adapted extract from *The Magic of Oz* by L Frank Baum (1856-1919).

© 2015 Stephen Curran

Now answer the following questions.

1) Why did Dorothy's friends need rescuing?

- [ ] a) Their feet were stuck to the ground.
- [ ] b) They were trapped on the toadstools.
- [ ] c) They were under the spell of the magic flower.
- [ ] d) The Wizard had cast a spell to restrain them.

2) What did the Wizard look like?

- [ ] a) He was short and stout.
- [ ] b) He was tall and wore a cape.
- [ ] c) He was small and bald-headed.
- [ ] d) He was lanky and red faced.

3) If the Wizard failed, what final option was available?

- [ ] a) Powder from the magic flower.
- [ ] b) Help from Glinda the Good Witch.
- [ ] c) Another magic tool from the bag.
- [ ] d) Finding the key to unlock Munchkin Country.

4) What was the most risky thing the Wizard did?

- [ ] a) The smoke he created nearly choked the captives.
- [ ] b) The sparks from his pistol ignited.
- [ ] c) He mixed hazardous powders together.
- [ ] d) He fired a gun and the shot just missed the young girl.

5) What equipment did the Wizard use to mix the potions?

- [ ] a) A silver bowl, tripod and powder
- [ ] b) A three-legged stand, bowl and vessel
- [ ] c) A vial, an easel and a pistol
- [ ] d) A basin, toadstool and flask

6) What does the word 'enveloped' (line 5) mean?

- [ ] a) Completely surrounded.
- [ ] b) Drifting like air.
- [ ] c) Wrapped up in a parcel.
- [ ] d) Covered in fog.

ae © 2015 Stephen Curran

7) How many times did the Wizard attempt to free the prisoners?

☐ a) Two
☐ b) Three
☐ c) A thousand
☐ d) The passage does not specify

8) What was Bill's profession?

☐ a) He was in the army.
☐ b) He was the expedition leader.
☐ c) He was a seafarer.
☐ d) He was the Munchkin's commander.

9) Which best describes this kind of narrative literature?

☐ a) Romantic legend
☐ b) Science fiction
☐ c) Fantasy story
☐ d) Mythic horror

10) Why was the Wizard so embarrassed once the hour had passed?

☐ a) Trot and Captain Bill could never be rescued.
☐ b) Dorothy had lost faith in his ability to solve the problem.
☐ c) He had forgotten to pack the magic tool he needed.
☐ d) Dorothy demanded he find the right key.

Fill in the missing letters to complete the passage.

Dinosaurs were on Earth for a period of 185 **11)** [m][ ][ ][l][ ][o][n] years, known **12)** [c][ ][l][ ][e][ ][t][ ][v][ ][l][y] as the Mesozoic era. Palaeontologists have proven, using fossil records, that birds are **13)** [ ][e][a][ ][h][e][ ][e][ ] dinosaurs, the only dinosaurs to survive the mass **14)** [ ][x][t][ ][n][c][ ][i][ ][n] event 66 million years ago. The term **15)** [d][ ][n][ ][s][ ][u][ ] comes from the Greek words 'deinos'

© 2015 Stephen Curran

16) m _ a _ _ _ g terrible and 'sauros' meaning lizard or reptile.

They were **17)** f _ r m _ l _ y named in 1842 by Sir Richard Owen, who wanted to show their **18)** i _ p r _ s _ i _ e size, but many have interpreted this name as showing the fearful

19) r e _ u _ a _ i o _ of the dinosaurs. There are two types of dinosaurs: **20)** c _ r _ i v _ r o _ s (meat-eating) and herbivorous (plant-eating).

Choose the word that means the same as the word on the left.

21)	**stay**	remain ☐	prompt ☐	leave ☐	recap ☐
22)	**cruel**	broth ☐	benevolent ☐	brutal ☐	blaming ☐
23)	**intense**	average ☐	strong ☐	risky ☐	terrible ☐
24)	**mix**	clash ☐	separate ☐	jar ☐	blend ☐
25)	**selfish**	selfless ☐	egotistical ☐	mussels ☐	altruistic ☐

Score ☐ **Percentage**

Verbal Activity Test 29

Read the following passage carefully.

<u>November 8th 1919</u>

On Father's and Dora's birthday Mother was so ill that we did not celebrate it at all. I was frightened that Mother was seriously ill, or even that… No, I won't even think it; one simply must not write it down even if one is not superstitious. Aunt Dora came last week to keep house for Mother. We are not going skating, for we are always afraid that Mother might get worse just when we are away. As soon as she is able to get up for long enough Father is going to take her to see a specialist doctor.

<u>November 16th</u>

Oh it's horrible, Mother has to have an operation; I'm so miserable that I can't write.

<u>November 19th</u>

Mother is so good and dear; she wants us to go skating to take our thoughts off the operation. But Dora says too that it would be brutal to go skating when Mother is going to have an operation in a few days.
Father said to us yesterday evening: "Pull yourselves together children and don't make things harder for your poor Mother."
But I can't help it, I cry whenever I look at Mother.

<u>November 23rd</u>

It is so dismal at home since Mother left; we had to go to school and believed she would not leave until the afternoon, but the carriage came in the morning. Dora says that Father had arranged it in this way because I could not control myself. Well, who could? Dora cries all day; and at school I cried a lot.

<u>November 28th</u>

Thank goodness, it's all over, Mother will be home again in a fortnight. I'm so happy and only now can I realise how horribly anxious I have been.

An adapted extract from *A Young Girl's Diary* by Anonymous.

Now answer the following questions.

1) On what date will Mother return home?

☐ a) 28th November

☐ b) 31st November

☐ c) 5th December

☐ d) 12th December

© 2015 Stephen Curran

2) What did the writer of the diary most fear?

- [ ] a) That they would not go skating.
- [ ] b) That her mother would die.
- [ ] c) That her mother's illness might persist.
- [ ] d) That they would never celebrate Dora's birthday.

3) What does 'superstitious' (line 5) mean in this context?

- [ ] a) The belief that particular actions can trigger good or bad luck.
- [ ] b) The belief in ghosts.
- [ ] c) A reliance on legends and myths.
- [ ] d) Being too sad to think it or write it down.

4) What suggests that Father and Dora could be twins?

- [ ] a) They are brother and sister.
- [ ] b) Dora helps her brother out.
- [ ] c) They share a birthday.
- [ ] d) Father and Dora are very close to each other.

5) On which day did Mother go to the hospital?

- [ ] a) November 16th
- [ ] b) November 19th
- [ ] c) November 23rd
- [ ] d) November 28th

6) Why does Father want everybody to stop crying?

- [ ] a) He does not like to see this girls upset.
- [ ] b) It is affecting their Mother.
- [ ] c) He does not want them to embarrass the family.
- [ ] d) It keeps Mother awake at night.

7) What fib did Father tell the girls?

- [ ] a) Mother would leave for hospital after they returned from school.
- [ ] b) Mother did not need an operation after all.
- [ ] c) Mother would only be away for one day.
- [ ] d) They would be allowed to accompany Mother to hospital.

© 2015 Stephen Curran

8) What activity did the adults suggest as a distraction for the girls?

- [ ] a) Writing a diary
- [ ] b) Crying
- [ ] c) Doing schoolwork
- [ ] d) Skating

9) What is the main purpose of this text?

- [ ] a) To explain
- [ ] b) To describe
- [ ] c) To entertain
- [ ] d) To persuade

10) What was the main purpose of Aunt Dora's visit?

- [ ] a) To comfort the children.
- [ ] b) To accompany Mother to hospital.
- [ ] c) To spend time with Father.
- [ ] d) To do the housekeeping.

Select the correct words to complete the passage.

John F Kennedy was the 35th **11)** [ ] president / [ ] king / [ ] emperor of the United States of America.

He was **12)** [ ] elected / [ ] voted / [ ] promoted in 1960 at the age of 43; the **13)** [ ] oldest / [ ] youngest / [ ] only man

ever to hold office. The main thing that JFK is known for is his

14) [ ] contraction / [ ] increase / [ ] expansion of the US space program. Kennedy **15)** [ ] pledged / [ ] promising / [ ] implied to

put the first man on the moon as part of the ongoing **16)** [ ] space / [ ] water / [ ] air race between

© 2015 Stephen Curran

America and Russia. Sadly, the president was **17)** [ ] assassinated / [ ] kidnapped / [ ] died on 22nd

November 1963 in Dallas, Texas before this became a **18)** [ ] truth / [ ] reality / [ ] factual in 1969.

He is **19)** [ ] forgotten / [ ] around / [ ] remembered today as one of the best-loved presidents in

20) [ ] history / [ ] forever / [ ] time .

Complete the word on the right so that it means the opposite of the word on the left.

21) **innocent**

	u			t	

22) **microscopic**

g		g			t	i	

23) **insolent**

r	e			e	c		f	u	

24) **insightful**

	n	p		r		e	p		i		e

25) **kindred**

u		r	e		a		e	

Score [ ] **Percentage** [ ] %

Verbal Activity Test 30

Read the following passage carefully.

October Snow

Swiftly the blizzard stretched a frozen arm
From out the hollow night--
Stripping the world of all her scarlet pomp,
And muffling her in white.

Dead white the hills; dead white the soundless plain;
Dead white the blizzard's breath--
Heavy with hoar that touched each woodland thing
With a white and silent death.

In inky stupor, along the drifted snow,
The sluggish river rolled--
A numb black snake caught lingering in the sun
By autumn's sudden cold.

By Lew Sarett (1888-1954).

Notes on Text:
hoar (line 7) - frost

Now answer the following questions.

1) What is the rhyming pattern of this poem?
- [ ] a) ABAB
- [ ] b) AABB
- [ ] c) ABCD
- [ ] d) ABCB

2) Which poetic technique is used in line 6?
- [ ] a) Metaphor
- [ ] b) Consonance
- [ ] c) Simile
- [ ] d) Assonance

© 2015 Stephen Curran

3) In which season does this poem occur?

- [ ] a) Spring
- [ ] b) Summer
- [ ] c) Autumn
- [ ] d) Winter

4) What is the river compared to?

- [ ] a) Ink-stained water
- [ ] b) A frozen limb
- [ ] c) A listless serpent
- [ ] d) A glistening sun

5) Which poetic technique is used in line 1?

- [ ] a) Assonance
- [ ] b) Personification
- [ ] c) Onomatopoeia
- [ ] d) Simile

6) How fast was the river flowing?

- [ ] a) Not at all
- [ ] b) Rapidly
- [ ] c) Normally
- [ ] d) Slowly

7) In which lines is anaphora used?

- [ ] a) Lines 1 and 3
- [ ] b) Lines 5 and 6
- [ ] c) Lines 4 and 11
- [ ] d) Lines 9 and 10

8) What mood does the poem convey?

- [ ] a) Bleak
- [ ] b) Cosy
- [ ] c) Bewildered
- [ ] d) Hopeful

ae © 2015 Stephen Curran

9) Which consonant sound is used most frequently in the third stanza?

- [ ] a) C
- [ ] b) R
- [ ] c) S
- [ ] d) B

10) What do the words 'dead' and 'death' imply about the scene (second stanza)?

- [ ] a) It was pristine.
- [ ] b) Everything was frozen.
- [ ] c) It was noiseless.
- [ ] d) Everything was dead.

Choose the correct words from the word bank to complete the passage.

A	twelve	B	Hades	C	Cronus	D	rule	E	overthrew
F	three	G	Olympian	H	sea	I	brothers	J	embodied

There were twelve **11)** ______________ gods, who were named after the place in which they lived: Mount Olympus (in modern-day Greece). Of these **12)** ______________, the three main gods were Zeus, Poseidon and Hades. Zeus **13)** ______________ their father, **14)** ______________, to end the rule of the Titans. After this act, the three **15)** ______________ drew lots in order to decide what proportion of the world each should **16)** ______________. Zeus won the draw and became king of the gods; Poseidon became god of the **17)** ______________; and **18)** ______________, the least liked of the **19)** ______________, became god of the underworld and of wealth, which **20)** ______________ his greed.

© 2015 Stephen Curran

Rearrange the words so that each sentence makes sense. Underline the word which does NOT fit into the sentence.

21) is hobbies the favourite after school guitar playing my activity

22) yesterday of Peter I had like flying if a dream Pan

23) fireworks therefore be night was it soon there will bonfire is

24) favourite my the is tonight movie television homework on

25) have been cue waiting queue hour the in half an I for

Score **Percentage**

Verbal Activity Test 31

Read the following passage carefully.

Scene: An old-fashioned garden.

[*Enter Nancy, a little girl of eight. She has a doll under one arm and a book under the other. She sits, puts her doll in the corner of the bench, and begins to talk to it.*]

NANCY: Sit there, Cynthia, and talk to me. You've got a silly expression today — don't pretend not to listen. I know you do hear, perfectly well. Are you listening? [*She makes the doll speak in a hurt voice.*]

CYNTHIA: Yes. But don't be cross with me!

NANCY [*Embracing her.*]: No, darling! Mother won't be cross with her dear Cynthia. That's right. Now you look a bright, intelligent child— like I have to look when I see Aunt Sophie. Now listen, Cynthia! I want to tell you something. It's a great secret. You won't tell anyone, will you?

CYNTHIA: Not even my friend?

NANCY [*Wagging her finger.*]: Certainly not! Do try to have a little sense, child! Not anyone! And especially not your friend. Do you understand? ... Very well! Now there's nothing to cry about. I shan't tell you if you cry... Now listen. I'm quite sure this is an enchanted garden?

CYNTHIA: Oh, Mother! Why?

NANCY [*Sternly.*]: You may well ask, my child! [*In her own voice.*] Because I had a lovely dream about it last night. I dreamt that all the people I want to be real people came into this garden, and were real people... Don't pretend you don't know what I mean, Cynthia! There's the little painted boy and girl on the teapot in the living room cabinet, and the flower fairy in that book Uncle Jack gave me, and the statue of the little boy with the bow and arrows in Uncle Jack's lobby.

An adapted extract from *The Enchanted Garden* by Netta Syrett (1865-1943).

Now answer the following questions.

1) What is the name of the doll?

☐ a) Aunt Sophie

☐ b) Cynthia

☐ c) Nancy

☐ d) Uncle Jack

© 2015 Stephen Curran

2) How does Nancy view her relationship with Cynthia?

- [ ] a) Nancy is her mother.
- [ ] b) Cynthia is her sister.
- [ ] c) They are good friends.
- [ ] d) Nancy is her aunt.

3) What does Nancy imagine will happen in the garden?

- [ ] a) Real people will not be allowed into the garden.
- [ ] b) She will have more dreams in the garden.
- [ ] c) She thinks characters will come to life.
- [ ] d) Nancy herself will become an imaginary character.

4) How many make-believe characters does Nancy dream about?

- [ ] a) Three
- [ ] b) Four
- [ ] c) Five
- [ ] d) Six

5) What impression does Nancy want Cynthia to convey to others?

- [ ] a) That Nancy is her only friend.
- [ ] b) That Cynthia is just like Nancy.
- [ ] c) That she is impertinent.
- [ ] d) That she only ever talks to Nancy.

6) What makes the doll cry?

- [ ] a) Nancy accuses the doll of having a stupid expression on her face.
- [ ] b) Nancy refuses to speak to the doll.
- [ ] c) The doll thinks she has upset Nancy.
- [ ] d) She is not allowed to tell her friend the secret.

7) What other activity might Nancy intend to do when she enters the garden?

- [ ] a) Read her book.
- [ ] b) Tend the flowers.
- [ ] c) Draw the flower fairy.
- [ ] d) Perform magical tricks.

ae © 2015 Stephen Curran

8) What is distinctive about this whole scene in the garden?

☐ a) All of the characters actually come to life.

☐ b) Nancy is portrayed as a foolish girl.

☐ c) Nancy has created an imaginary world.

☐ d) Nancy has lots of secrets.

9) What are the only other locations mentioned inside the house?

☐ a) The kitchen and the garden.

☐ b) The lounge and the hallway.

☐ c) The lobby and the attic.

☐ d) The sitting room and the library.

10) How do we know that Nancy trusts Cynthia?

☐ a) She is her only friend.

☐ b) She says she does not trust Aunt Sophie or Uncle Jack.

☐ c) She confides in her.

☐ d) Only Cynthia listens to her.

Complete the word on the right so that it means the opposite of the word on the left.

11) **solitary**

s		c			b	l	

12) **winning**

l					g

13) **willingness**

	e	l	u		t		n	c	

14) **ignite**

e		t	i		g			s	

15) **opaque**

	r		n			a	r		n	t

© 2015 Stephen Curran

Four of the words in each list are linked. Mark the rectangle under the word that is NOT related to these four.

16)	boulder	cardholder	folder	bodybuilder	moulder
17)	puck	sprite	pixie	centaur	imp
18)	stomach	beseeched	chlorine	technical	anchor
19)	atrocious	winsome	fetching	charming	pleasant
20)	bronze	chocolate	mahogany	sienna	indigo

Choose the word that means the same as the word on the left.

21) **sadness**	calamity	sorrow	rage	setback
22) **unfair**	biased	direct	moral	exposed
23) **popular**	despised	rare	shunned	common
24) **renovate**	transfer	rearrange	improvise	restore
25) **loathsome**	willing	amusing	despicable	boring

Score **Percentage**

© 2015 Stephen Curran

Verbal Activity Test 32

Read the following passage carefully.

You are old, Father William

"You are old, Father William," the young man said,
"And your hair has become very white;
And yet you incessantly stand on your head –
Do you think, at your age, it is right?"

"In my youth," Father William replied to his son,
"I feared it might injure the brain;
But, now that I'm perfectly sure I have none,
Why, I do it again and again."

"You are old," said the youth, "as I mentioned before,
And have grown most uncommonly fat;
Yet you turned a back-somersault in at the door –
Pray, what is the reason of that?"

"In my youth," said the sage, as he shook his grey locks,
"I kept all my limbs very supple
By the use of this ointment – one shilling the box –
Allow me to sell you a couple?"

"You are old," said the youth, "and your jaws are too weak
For anything tougher than suet;
Yet you finished the goose, with the bones and the beak –
Pray, how did you manage to do it?"

"In my youth," said his father, "I took to the law,
And argued each case with my wife;
And the muscular strength, which it gave to my jaw,
Has lasted the rest of my life."

"You are old," said the youth, "one would hardly suppose
That your eye was as steady as ever;
Yet you balanced an eel on the end of your nose –
What made you so awfully clever?"

"I have answered three questions, and that is enough,"
Said his father; "don't give yourself airs!
Do you think I can listen all day to such stuff?
Be off, or I'll kick you downstairs!"

By Lewis Carroll (1832-1898).

© 2015 Stephen Curran

Now answer the following questions.

1) What is the rhyming pattern of each stanza?

- [ ] a) ABAB
- [ ] b) ABBA
- [ ] c) ABCB
- [ ] d) ABCD

2) What acrobatic activities can Father William perform?

- [ ] a) Cartwheels and balancing acts
- [ ] b) Forward rolls and handstands
- [ ] c) Headstands and flips
- [ ] d) Handsprings and tightrope walking

3) Throughout the poem, 'You are old' and 'In my youth' are examples of which poetic technique?

- [ ] a) Consonance
- [ ] b) Anaphora
- [ ] c) Onomatopoeia
- [ ] d) Hyperbole

4) How many questions does the son ask his father?

- [ ] a) One
- [ ] b) Two
- [ ] c) Three
- [ ] d) Four

5) What is the meaning of 'don't give yourself airs!' (line 30)?

- [ ] a) Do not ask adults important questions.
- [ ] b) Do not daydream.
- [ ] c) Do not be disrespectful to an adult.
- [ ] d) Do not listen to adults.

6) What did Father William use ointment for?

- [ ] a) To ease his back pain.
- [ ] b) To maintain his flexibility.
- [ ] c) To stop his hair from going white.
- [ ] d) To grease his jaw.

© 2015 Stephen Curran

7) What is the mood and tone of this poem?

- [ ] a) Humorous
- [ ] b) Serious
- [ ] c) Cheerful
- [ ] d) Gloomy

8) What is the theme of this poem?

- [ ] a) The relationship between a father and his son.
- [ ] b) The loss of faculties in old age.
- [ ] c) Youthful impertinence.
- [ ] d) Defying the aging process.

9) What was the appearance of the old man?

- [ ] a) He was short and wore glasses.
- [ ] b) He had a strong jaw and dark hair.
- [ ] c) He was overweight with greying hair.
- [ ] d) He had bright eyes and was thin.

10) Which structural technique is used at the end of line 17?

- [ ] a) End of stanza
- [ ] b) Enjambment
- [ ] c) Punctuation
- [ ] d) Caesura

Choose the correct words from the word bank to complete the passage.

A	wooden	B	rank	C	stone	D	victory	E	Prague
F	protection	G	built	H	England	I	size	J	introduced

Large, strong castles were often **11)** ______________ by important people to provide **12)** ______________ from attack to the inhabitants within. The first castles were **13)** ______________ to **14)** ______________ by the Normans

© 2015 Stephen Curran

after their **15)** ______________ at the Battle of Hastings, in 1066. Castles were built nationwide for nearly 500 years. The first type of castle that was built was the **16)** ______________ Motte and Bailey. These were subsequently replaced by permanent **17)** ______________ castles. The **18)** ______________ of each fortress displayed the owner's **19)** ______________ and wealth. The greatest castle in England is Windsor Castle, however the largest castle in the world is **20)** ______________ Castle.

Rearrange the words so that each sentence makes sense. Underline the word which does NOT fit into the sentence.

21) the is I school to to to bag really heavy take need

22) very went I the today farmer busy market was to

23) television to recording a show of see a went of we

24) is fable a to there moral every are

25) my in end holidays in start September summer May and at

Score ☐ **Percentage** ☐ %

Verbal Activity Test 33

Read the following passage carefully.

Jousting was a medieval sport where two armoured opponents on horseback charged at each other with lances in order to dismount the other rider. King Henry VIII (June 1491 – January 1547) was very fond of jousting tournaments but, as he grew older, his desire to compete often came at the expense of his health. Henry's injuries may have contributed to bad headaches and a short temper. The following incident occurred on 10th March 1524.

The Duke of Suffolk, Charles Brandon, charged forward with his lance, and the king likewise unadvisedly set off towards the duke.

The people, seeing the king's bare face, cried "Hold, hold!" The duke neither saw nor heard, and whether the king remembered his visor was up or not few could tell. The lance struck the king on the brow, right under the guard of his headpiece. The blow pushed Henry's visor so far back that his helmet was full of splinters. The people were aghast that the duke may have blinded the king or seriously wounded him.

Charles immediately disarmed and went over to the king, to ensure Henry could still see. Then he vowed that he would never again run against his sovereign. Even if the king was hurt just a little, the armourers or the duke would be blamed. Fortunately, the king got up and laughed off the incident. He stated that no one was to blame but himself, for he was not seriously hurt and his sight was not damaged. Then Henry called his armourers to gather all his pieces of armour together, took a lance and jousted six more times very well. All could see that he was not injured, which was a great joy and comfort to all his subjects present.

An adapted extract from an account by George Cavendish (1497-1562), Cardinal Wolsey's servant.

Now answer the following questions.

1) How old was Henry when the accident occurred?

☐ a) 30

☐ b) 31

☐ c) 32

☐ d) 33

© 2015 Stephen Curran

2) How many years and months after the incident did Henry die?

- [ ] a) 22 years and 10 months
- [ ] b) 23 years and 2 months
- [ ] c) 22 years and 2 months
- [ ] d) 23 years and 10 months

3) How many times does this account say the king jousted on that day?

- [ ] a) 5
- [ ] b) 6
- [ ] c) 7
- [ ] d) 8

4) What should the king have been told before the joust?

- [ ] a) His eye guard was not in place.
- [ ] b) The Duke of Suffolk was not ready.
- [ ] c) Jousting was too dangerous for a king.
- [ ] d) His helmet was broken.

5) What did Henry sacrifice for his love of the sport?

- [ ] a) Governing the country effectively.
- [ ] b) His physical wellbeing.
- [ ] c) The respect of his subjects.
- [ ] d) His friendship with Charles.

6) What did the Duke of Suffolk fear had happened as a result of the incident?

- [ ] a) The king had been killed.
- [ ] b) He had lost the king's trust.
- [ ] c) The king had lost his sight.
- [ ] d) The king's armour had been damaged.

7) What did Charles promise?

- [ ] a) A rematch against the king.
- [ ] b) He would never joust again.
- [ ] c) He would always check the king's attire personally before jousting.
- [ ] d) He would never joust against the king again.

ae © 2015 Stephen Curran

8) What does this incident suggest about the power the king held?

- [ ] a) Henry had absolute power.
- [ ] b) Henry allowed his advisers to make big decisions for him.
- [ ] c) His dukes shared power with him.
- [ ] d) His subjects were allowed to vote on important issues.

9) Where did the duke's lance hit the king?

- [ ] a) On his chest
- [ ] b) In his eye
- [ ] c) On his forehead
- [ ] d) On his cheek

10) What was the king's attitude towards the incident?

- [ ] a) He was extremely angry.
- [ ] b) He made light of it.
- [ ] c) He blamed everyone around him.
- [ ] d) He was amused at the duke's poor aim.

Choose the word that means the same as the word on the left.

11) **punctual**	tardy ☐	hole ☐	prompt ☐	inflate ☐
12) **taint**	contaminate ☐	improve ☐	dye ☐	clean ☐
13) **ominous**	promising ☐	threatening ☐	dark ☐	unhappy ☐
14) **scoundrel**	scrub ☐	rogue ☐	noisy ☐	champion ☐
15) **lessen**	fasten ☐	magnify ☐	fewer ☐	diminish ☐

© 2015 Stephen Curran

Complete the word on the right so that it means the same as, or nearly the same as, the word on the left.

16) **manipulative**

s		h		m		n	

17) **gifted**

	a	l		n		e	

18) **envisage**

f		r		s		e

19) **depressed**

	n	h		p		y

20) **euphoric**

o		e	r		o			d

Choose the word that has a similar meaning to the words in both sets of brackets.

21) (obstruct, impede) (stand, table) — hinder stall booth thwart bench

22) (incantation, charm) (interval, season) — spell hiatus chant term summons

23) (joke, tease) (goat, billy) — jest mock hoax taunt kid

24) (drake, waterbird) (bend, crouch) — stoop squat crook duck bow

25) (tie, join) (cluster, group) — muster huddle knot seam collect

Score **Percentage**

© 2015 Stephen Curran

Verbal Activity Test 34

Read the following passage carefully.

The French Emperor Napoleon Bonaparte (August 1769 - May 1821) conquered most of Europe in the early 19th century. He was defeated at the Battle of Waterloo in Belgium on 18 June 1815. The last charge of the British Army is described by 21-year-old Captain Gronow:

At five o'clock we received orders to retire behind an elevation at our rear. The enemy's artillery had come up en masse only a hundred yards away. As they discharged their guns, we were face downwards behind the rising ground, and protected by the ridge.

The enemy's cavalry was behind their artillery, to protect it if attacked; but we made no attempt to do so. We heard the non-stop boom of artillery, accompanied by the incessant rattling echoes of musketry. After half an hour, the brutal pounding ceased and the whole Imperial infantry of the Guard attacked, led by the Emperor himself. We now had roughly 20,000 of the best soldiers in France before us, the heroes of many memorable victories. We saw their bearskin caps rising higher and higher as they ascended the ridge of ground which separated us, and advanced nearer to our lines.

At this moment the Duke of Wellington gave his famous order for our bayonet charge. He rode along the line, shouting, 'Guards, get up and charge!' We were relieved and stood up immediately as we had been irritated by so many hours of inaction and defensive positioning. The fighting spirit of the officers and men was very high because they had lost so many of their comrades and friends earlier in the battle. Our infantry fired a volley as soon as the enemy were within shot and we rushed at them with fixed bayonets screaming "Hurrah!"

An adapted extract from *The Reminiscences and Recollections of Captain Gronow* by RH Gronow (1794–1865).

Notes on Text:
en masse (line 2) – in a group, all together
musketry (line 7) – gunfire

© 2015 Stephen Curran

Now answer the following questions.

1) Who led the charge of the Imperial infantry?
- ☐ a) The French cavalry
- ☐ b) Napoleon Bonaparte
- ☐ c) Captain Gronow
- ☐ d) Duke of Wellington

2) What indication did the British have that the French were approaching?
- ☐ a) There was a pause in the gunfire.
- ☐ b) They heard the command to charge.
- ☐ c) They saw the tops of their hats.
- ☐ d) Volleys of shots were fired.

3) At what time did the French foot soldiers attack?
- ☐ a) 5.30pm
- ☐ b) 5 o'clock
- ☐ c) 20:00
- ☐ d) 9.00pm

4) Where were the British troops stationed?
- ☐ a) On top of a hill.
- ☐ b) Behind the artillery.
- ☐ c) On open ground.
- ☐ d) Behind the crest of a hill.

5) In what state of readiness were the British troops?
- ☐ a) Standing in lines
- ☐ b) On horseback
- ☐ c) At attention
- ☐ d) Lying down

6) How old was Napoleon at the Battle of Waterloo?
- ☐ a) 21
- ☐ b) 45
- ☐ c) 46
- ☐ d) 51

© 2015 Stephen Curran

7) What did the Duke of Wellington order his troops to do?

- [ ] a) Run at the enemy with fixed bayonets.
- [ ] b) Fire a volley.
- [ ] c) Make a cavalry charge.
- [ ] d) Take up defensive positioning.

8) How did Captain Gronow and his men feel when they went into battle?

- [ ] a) Tired and irritated
- [ ] b) Hopeless but calm
- [ ] c) Energised and vengeful
- [ ] d) Fearful but determined

9) What gunpowder weaponry was being used?

- [ ] a) Rifles and muskets
- [ ] b) Guns and swords
- [ ] c) Cannons and daggers
- [ ] d) Bayonets and spears

10) Where was the French cavalry positioned?

- [ ] a) One hundred yards behind the guns.
- [ ] b) To the rear of the enemy artillery.
- [ ] c) In front of the 20,000 French soldiers.
- [ ] d) Behind the ridge.

Complete the word on the right so that it means the opposite of the word on the left.

11) **terrific**

	r		a		f	u	

12) **defensive**

a	g		r			s	i		e

13) **wise**

	o		l	i		

14) **solemn**

c		e	e			u	

15) **quirky**

c		n		e	n		i	o		a	

© 2015 Stephen Curran

Choose the word that has a similar meaning to the words in both sets of brackets.

16) (upland, heath) (secure, anchor) — fortify affix fell moor highland

17) (period, term) (flavour, spice) — era season zest phase colour

18) (pelvis, waist) (trendy, fashionable) — belly cool abdomen chic hip

19) (stem, trunk) (trail, shadow) — shoot follow stalk crate tail

20) (tuft, snippet) (secure, fasten) — lock safe morsel join clump

Four of the words in each list are linked. Mark the rectangle under the word that is NOT related to these four.

21)	Scorpio	Aries	Leo	Gemini	Earth
22)	tenet	lever	minim	level	dewed
23)	reprimand	criticise	scold	chastise	exalt
24)	flexible	taut	supple	bendable	lithe
25)	fusilli	bolognese	penne	spaghetti	lasagne

Score ____ Percentage ____ %

© 2015 Stephen Curran

Verbal Activity Test 35

Read the following passage carefully.

The Owl

1

When cats run home and light is come,
And dew is cold upon the ground,
And the far-off stream is dumb,
And the whirring sail goes round,
And the whirring sail goes round;
Alone and warming his five wits,
The white owl in the belfry sits.

2

When merry milkmaids click the latch,
And rarely smells the new-mown hay,
And the cock hath sung beneath the thatch
Twice or thrice his roundelay,
Twice or thrice his roundelay;
Alone and warming his five wits,
The white owl in the belfry sits.

By Lord Alfred Tennyson (1809-1892).

Now answer the following questions.

1) Which sound device is being used in the word 'click' (line 8)?
- ☐ a) Onomatopoeia
- ☐ b) Assonance
- ☐ c) Alliteration
- ☐ d) Consonance

2) How many times does the poet use identical phrase anaphora in successive lines?
- ☐ a) Once
- ☐ b) Twice
- ☐ c) Three times
- ☐ d) Four times

© 2015 Stephen Curran

3) What do you think 'roundelay' (line 11) means?

- [ ] a) To fly in a circle.
- [ ] b) The hooting of the owl.
- [ ] c) A simple song and refrain.
- [ ] d) The plumpness of the cockerel.

4) At what time of day does the poem take place?

- [ ] a) Dawn
- [ ] b) Midday
- [ ] c) Dusk
- [ ] d) Night

5) What does the 'whirring sail' (line 4) signify?

- [ ] a) Ships docking into harbour.
- [ ] b) The movement of a windmill.
- [ ] c) A metaphor for the flight of the owl.
- [ ] d) Billowing fabric of a ship under sail.

6) What does the metaphor 'warming his five wits' (lines 6 & 13) mean?

- [ ] a) Thinking wise thoughts about the world he surveys.
- [ ] b) Using his feathers to keep his talons warm.
- [ ] c) Preparing himself to hunt for prey.
- [ ] d) Waking up and feeling cold.

7) What is the rhyming pattern of this poem?

- [ ] a) ABAABCC
- [ ] b) ABABBCC
- [ ] c) ABABCCB
- [ ] d) ABBAACC

8) What is a 'belfry' (line 7)?

- [ ] a) A barn.
- [ ] b) The roof of a house.
- [ ] c) An aged tree.
- [ ] d) A bell tower.

9) What do you think 'the far-off stream is dumb' (line 3) suggests?

- [ ] a) The stream does not speak.
- [ ] b) The stream has no fish.
- [ ] c) The stream is frozen.
- [ ] d) The owl cannot hear the stream.

10) What mood does this poem convey?

- [ ] a) Peace and tranquillity
- [ ] b) Fear and anxiety
- [ ] c) Restless and moody
- [ ] d) Lonely and chaotic

Choose the word that means the opposite of the word on the left.

11) **critical**	serious ☐	stable ☐	grave ☐	important ☐
12) **genuine**	authentic ☐	spirit ☐	honest ☐	fake ☐
13) **unite**	connect ☐	fasten ☐	divide ☐	return ☐
14) **extravagant**	thrifty ☐	excessive ☐	quiet ☐	ornate ☐
15) **principled**	righteous ☐	mistaken ☐	just ☐	unethical ☐

Choose the word that has a similar meaning to the words in both sets of brackets.

16) (caring, gentle) (sore, painful) — tender lesion affectionate raw placid

17) (nurture, parent) (end, back) — raise reverse rear foster remnant

© 2015 Stephen Curran

18) (condition, shape) (country, nation) — realm form republic state order

19) (shower, barrage) (praise, acclaim) — deluge hail torrent honour onslaught

20) (feat, trick) (inhibit, hinder) — deter exploit hamper deed stunt

Choose the word that means the same as the word on the left.

21) **frailty**	quality ☐	intensity ☐	solidity ☐	infirmity ☐
22) **treacherous**	safe ☐	disloyal ☐	faithful ☐	expected ☐
23) **wishy-washy**	decisive ☐	cheap ☐	weak ☐	rough ☐
24) **integrate**	combine ☐	separate ☐	extract ☐	detach ☐
25) **rancorous**	excusing ☐	bitter ☐	civil ☐	sickly ☐

Score ☐ **Percentage**

© 2015 Stephen Curran

Verbal Activity Test 36

Read the following passage carefully.

The young d'Artagnan travelled to Paris to join the Musketeers of the Guard. At the Musketeer's headquarters, he insulted three formidable musketeers: Athos, Porthos and Aramis.

Gallantly, d'Artagnan drew his sword. Blood had gone to his head and at that moment he would have fought against all the Musketeers in the kingdom. It was a quarter past midday. The sun was at its zenith over the spot chosen for the duel.

"It's very hot," said Athos, drawing his sword, "and I can't take off my doublet. My wound is bleeding again and I wouldn't like to annoy Monsieur with the sight of blood which he has not drawn from me himself."

"That's true, Monsieur," replied d'Artagnan, "and whether drawn by myself or another, I assure you I always view with regret the blood of so brave a gentleman. I will therefore fight in my doublet too."

"Come, enough of such compliments!" cried Porthos. "Remember, we're waiting our turn."

"Speak for yourself!" interrupted Aramis. " I think what they say is very well said and quite worthy of two gentlemen."

"When you're ready, Monsieur," said Athos, putting himself on guard.

"I await your orders," said d'Artagnan, crossing swords.

Scarcely had the two rapiers clashed, when Cardinal Richelieu's Guard, accompanied by their captain, arrived.

"Sheathe your swords, gentlemen!" cried Aramis and Porthos simultaneously.

But it was too late. The two combatants had been seen with their weapons raised. Athos, Porthos and Aramis regrouped, while the captain drew up his soldiers.

"There are five of them," whispered Athos, "and we're but three; we'll be beaten again."

"Gentlemen," said d'Artagnan, "allow me to correct your words. You said you were but three, but it appears to me we are four."

And the fight commenced.

An adapted extract from *The Three Musketeers* by Alexandre Dumas (1802-1870).

Notes on Text:
doublet (line 6) - a padded jacket

© 2015 Stephen Curran

Now answer the following questions.

1) What does it mean when d'Artagnan's 'blood had gone to his head' (line 1)?

- [ ] a) He was feeling hot.
- [ ] b) He was angry.
- [ ] c) He was embarrassed.
- [ ] d) He was feeling unwell.

2) What are 'rapiers' (line 17)?

- [ ] a) Shields
- [ ] b) Combatants
- [ ] c) Blades
- [ ] d) Spears

3) Which two people were about to fight each other first?

- [ ] a) d'Artagnan and Athos
- [ ] b) Portos and d'Artagnan
- [ ] c) d'Artagnan and Aramis
- [ ] d) Athos and Aramis

4) What was the overall tone of the Musketeers' conversation?

- [ ] a) Serious
- [ ] b) Insulting
- [ ] c) Tense
- [ ] d) Jesting

5) At what time was the fight to take place?

- [ ] a) 12.15am
- [ ] b) 12.15pm
- [ ] c) 11.45am
- [ ] d) 00:15

6) What does the word 'zenith' (line 3) mean?

- [ ] a) Peak
- [ ] b) Lowest
- [ ] c) Midpoint
- [ ] d) When it is visible

ae © 2015 Stephen Curran

7) What was d'Artagnan's attitude towards the three musketeers?

☐ a) Dismissive
☐ b) Fearful
☐ c) Respectful
☐ d) Indifferent

8) Why did Athos leave his doublet on?

☐ a) He was fashion conscious.
☐ b) He was injured.
☐ c) He wanted to be in a proper state of dress.
☐ d) He was cold.

9) How many people engaged in the fight?

☐ a) Four
☐ b) Five
☐ c) Eight
☐ d) Nine

10) How did the three musketeers intend to deal with d'Artagnan?

☐ a) Leave it to Athos.
☐ b) All together.
☐ c) One after the other.
☐ d) Have him arrested by Cardinal Richelieu.

Choose the correct words from the word bank to complete the passage.

A	desert	B	prince	C	fulfil	D	pyramid	E	disregarded
F	suddenly	G	mighty	H	brothers	I	continually	J	becoming

There was once an Egyptian **11)** ______________ called Thutmose, who had many **12)** ______________ and half-brothers who **13)** ______________ plotted against him. This worried him and consequently he often **14)** ______________ his

© 2015 Stephen Curran

responsibilities and went into the **15)** ______________. On one of these trips, he visited the **16)** ______________ pyramid of the Pharaoh Khafra. At the foot of this **17)** ______________ was a colossal carving of Harmachis, the god of the rising sun. Thutmose prayed to Harmachis and **18)** ______________ the statue came to life. The statue told him to **19)** ______________ his duty and become Pharaoh, which he did, **20)** ______________ one of the greatest kings of Egypt.

Rearrange the words so that each sentence makes sense. Underline the word which does NOT fit into the sentence.

21) the woke up bus I trainers missed late and

22) game bowling this party I my birthday for year a had

23) is favourite it is my mouse the animal elephant enormous because

24) the has very shop a busy days week it for been

25) milky like a sugars please would hate two I tea with

Score ______ Percentage ______ %

Verbal Activity Test 37

Read the following passage carefully.

With the Eagle

His eye
Sweeps all the sky,
As hard he grips the rock.
Storm's ice-clad brood that round him flock
But blow the fires of his undaunted breast,
And forth he fares in ecstasy of quest.
Still up he goes, to proudly fling
His own against the thunder's wing.
O Eagle of the mighty heart,
Your strength in me impart:
Breed in my soul your lofty air,
That it may nobly dare,
And with unconquerable will
Face every darkest ill.

An adaptation of a poem by Edward Robeson Taylor (1838-1923).

<u>Notes on Text:</u>
brood (line 4) - offspring
ecstasy (line 6) - overwhelming happiness

Now answer the following questions.

1) What rhyming pattern is used in this poem?
- [ ] a) Rhyming triplets
- [ ] b) Every other line
- [ ] c) Rhyming couplets
- [ ] d) First and fourth line rhyming

2) What is the eagle's most likely 'quest' (line 6)?
- [ ] a) To protect his young.
- [ ] b) To fly as low to the ground as he can.
- [ ] c) To enjoy the warm weather.
- [ ] d) To hunt for prey.

© 2015 Stephen Curran

3) What type of verse is this poem?

- [ ] a) Formal verse
- [ ] b) Free verse
- [ ] c) Blank verse
- [ ] d) Haiku

4) What does the phrase 'to proudly fling / His own against the thunder's wing' (lines 7 & 8) mean?

- [ ] a) His wings are as powerful as thunder.
- [ ] b) He is no match for the strong wind.
- [ ] c) His wings make the sounds of thunder.
- [ ] d) He is flying in a winter storm.

5) What quality does the poet want to develop that the eagle displays?

- [ ] a) A lack of mercy for others.
- [ ] b) Bravery in the face of difficulty.
- [ ] c) The ability to nurture his family.
- [ ] d) Learning to hunt like an eagle.

6) Which poetic technique is most prominent in lines 5 and 6?

- [ ] a) Alliteration
- [ ] b) Assonance
- [ ] c) Onomatopoeia
- [ ] d) Anaphora

7) What is the eagle doing at the beginning of the poem?

- [ ] a) Sleeping
- [ ] b) Feeding his chicks.
- [ ] c) Surveying his surroundings.
- [ ] d) Flying

8) In which line does the emphasis of the poem change?

- [ ] a) Line 6
- [ ] b) Line 9
- [ ] c) Line 10
- [ ] d) Line 13

© 2015 Stephen Curran

9) Where is the eagle at the start of the poem?

- ☐ a) At ground level.
- ☐ b) In a tree.
- ☐ c) On an ice shelf.
- ☐ d) High up in a cliff face.

10) What does the word 'undaunted' (line 5) mean?

- ☐ a) Fearless
- ☐ b) Intimidated
- ☐ c) Hungry
- ☐ d) Vicious

Choose the word that means the same as the word on the left.

11) **fresh**	mature ☐	crisp ☐	tired ☐	musty ☐
12) **strong**	faint ☐	robotic ☐	flimsy ☐	robust ☐
13) **ingenuous**	innocent ☐	smart ☐	dishonest ☐	prodigy ☐
14) **diligent**	idle ☐	ideally ☐	industrious ☐	indicate ☐
15) **placid**	calm ☐	anxious ☐	horizontal ☐	leaden ☐

Complete the word on the right so that it means the opposite of the word on the left.

16) **scrumptious**

	e	v		l		i		g

17) **reckless**

c		u	t			u	s

18) **respectful**

d	i		d	a		n	f		l

© 2015 Stephen Curran

19)	**docile**	s		u		b	o		n
20)	**ruthless**	m	e		c		f	u	

Four of the words in each list are linked. Mark the rectangle under the word that is NOT related to these four.

21)	original	unique	novel	legend	innovative
22)	crossword	fjord	toward	aboard	chord
23)	kayak	canoe	stern	gondola	punt
24)	gangster	foreign	campaign	gnome	consignment
25)	delete	remove	erase	inject	obliterate

Score Percentage

© 2015 Stephen Curran

Verbal Activity Test 38

Read the following passage carefully.

The story is told by Axel, a student whose uncle, the German professor, Otto Lidenbrock, believes there are volcanic tubes reaching the centre of the Earth. They and their guide, Hans, descend into an Icelandic volcano and experience many adventures that involve encounters with prehistoric animals and natural hazards.

At about midday our guide Hans prepared and baited a hook, and cast the line into the subterranean waters. The bait he used was a small piece of meat, which concealed the hook. I was anxious for a long time and prepared myself for disappointment. Were these waters supplied with fish or not? I thought it was unlikely. Then there came a sudden and rather hard tug. Hans coolly drew the line in, and with it the catch, which struggled violently to escape.

"A fish!" exclaimed my uncle.

"It's a sturgeon!" I cried.

The Professor carefully examined the fish's characteristics and his opinion contradicted mine. The fish had a flat head, round body, and its bottom half was covered with bony scales; it had no teeth, the pectoral fins sprouted direct from the body and it did not have a tail. The animal certainly belonged to the sturgeon family, but it differed from that fish in many ways.

My uncle was not mistaken. After lengthy and patient examination, he stated, "This fish, my dear boy, belongs to a species which is extinct and of which no trace has ever been found on earth, except in fossil remains."

"Are you saying," I cried, "that we have captured a live specimen of a fish that existed before the Great Flood?"

"Yes, we have!" announced the Professor, "To hold this living specimen in one's hand is enough to make a naturalist happy for life."

An adapted extract from *Journey to the Centre of the Earth* by Jules Verne (1828-1905).

Notes on Text:
Great Flood (line 18) - many archaeologists believe there is evidence for a cataclysmic flood event in pre-historic times

© 2015 Stephen Curran

Now answer the following questions.

1) Why was the event described in this passage so important?
- [ ] a) They had discovered fish under the earth.
- [ ] b) They had found a food source.
- [ ] c) They had discovered an extinct species was still alive.
- [ ] d) They had discovered a fish that was common on earth.

2) What does 'extinct' (line 15) mean?
- [ ] a) The animals in that species no longer exist.
- [ ] b) The species thrives in some parts of the earth.
- [ ] c) Uncovered bones of a pre-historic species.
- [ ] d) The species never existed at all.

3) What is meant by 'subterranean' (line 2)?
- [ ] a) An underwater vessel.
- [ ] b) Below the surface of the Earth.
- [ ] c) A flowing river.
- [ ] d) Beneath the surface of a river.

4) What is a naturalist (line 20)?
- [ ] a) A scientific expert on living things.
- [ ] b) Someone who disregards nature.
- [ ] c) An admirer of nature.
- [ ] d) Someone who wants to eliminate species.

5) What did they use the portion of animal flesh for?
- [ ] a) To cook for lunch.
- [ ] b) To check if the sturgeon ate meat.
- [ ] c) As a raw snack for the journey.
- [ ] d) To lure the fish.

6) What did they think had destroyed all of the pre-historic creatures?
- [ ] a) More powerful species.
- [ ] b) A huge deluge.
- [ ] c) Human beings.
- [ ] d) A big explosion.

ae © 2015 Stephen Curran

7) What relation is Axel to Professor Lidenbrock?

- [ ] a) His uncle
- [ ] b) His brother
- [ ] c) His nephew
- [ ] d) His son

8) How did the fish differ from a normal sturgeon?

- [ ] a) It had a flat head.
- [ ] b) It had bony scales.
- [ ] c) It had a tail.
- [ ] d) It is not stated.

9) How do you think the professor felt about his discovery?

- [ ] a) Euphoric
- [ ] b) Unsure
- [ ] c) Disturbed
- [ ] d) Pleased

10) In which country did their journey begin?

- [ ] a) Germany
- [ ] b) Antarctica
- [ ] c) Iceland
- [ ] d) Subterranean Earth

Select the correct words to complete the passage.

Centrepoint is a **11)** [ ] charity / [ ] palace / [ ] street for homeless people between the ages of sixteen and twenty-five. The charity helps them with housing, health care and

12) [ ] education / [ ] school / [ ] flats, with many workers and **13)** [ ] prince / [ ] volunteers / [ ] helping working around

© 2015 Stephen Curran ae

the **14)** [ ] people / [ ] world / [ ] clock in the North-east of England, Greater London and Bradford.

They are supported by many **15)** [ ] different / [ ] variety / [ ] mixture people and **16)** [ ] adjectives / [ ] collection / [ ] collectives ,

from football clubs and global banks to TV shows and community organisations.

The charity works with a **17)** [ ] wide / [ ] long / [ ] high range of people to raise

18) [ ] money / [ ] awareness / [ ] ideas and funds. The Duke of Cambridge became a

19) [ ] unobservant / [ ] keen / [ ] ideal patron for Centrepoint in 2005, eager to continue the

20) [ ] unhelpful / [ ] successfully / [ ] wonderful work of his mother, Princess Diana.

Complete the word on the right so that it means the same as, or nearly the same as, the word on the left.

21)	**saintly**	v		r		u	o		s		
22)	**reliant**	d	e		e		d	a	n		
23)	**boisterous**		n	i	m	a		e			
24)	**wonderful**	m	a		v		l		o		s
25)	**personal**		n		i	v		d	u		l

Score [ ] **Percentage** [%]

Verbal Activity Test 39

Read the following passage carefully.

Malala Yousafzai was born on 12th July 1997 in the Swat Valley in north-west Pakistan. Her family ran a chain of local schools and she grew up believing that Pakistani girls should have the same right to education as boys. The Taliban, an extreme fundamentalist political grouping, had banned girls from attending school in Malala's neighbourhood.

In 2009, Yousafzai wrote a blog for the BBC describing the Taliban's influence in the Swat Valley and her views on female education. The following year, the Pakistani army took military action against the Taliban, just as the New York Times made a documentary about Malala. She was featured in the worldwide media and nominated for the International Children's Peace Prize.

The Taliban issued a death threat against Malala, but her father did not believe they would hurt a child. On 9th October 2012, Malala got on her school bus. A gunman climbed aboard asking for her and when her friends glanced at Malala, he fired three pistol shots at her. A bullet hit Malala in the left side of her forehead, leaving her seriously injured. After extensive surgery in Pakistan, she was transported while in a coma to a hospital in Birmingham, England, for intensive rehabilitation.

The assassination attempt sparked an international outpouring of support. A German broadcaster wrote in 2013 that Malala had become 'the most famous teenager in the world'. From 2013, Time magazine featured Malala for three years running as one of 'The 100 Most Influential People in the World.' In July of that year, she spoke at the United Nations headquarters to call for worldwide access to education. Among the many prizes and honours she has received, Yousafzai became the youngest-ever Nobel Peace Prize laureate at the age of 17.

Notes on Text:
fundamentalist (line 4) – one who interprets religious texts literally
laureate (line 24) - a person who is honoured with an award

Now answer the following questions.

1) Which media outlet first brought attention to Malala?

☐ a) Time magazine

☐ b) A German broadcaster

☐ c) The BBC

☐ d) New York Times

© 2015 Stephen Curran

2) What was significant about Malala's receipt of the Nobel Peace Prize?

- [ ] a) She was the only young person to ever to be nominated.
- [ ] b) She was the bravest teenager to ever receive the award.
- [ ] c) She is the only advocate for worldwide education.
- [ ] d) She is the youngest teenage recipient of the prize.

3) How old was Malala when the assassination attempt occurred?

- [ ] a) 14
- [ ] b) 15
- [ ] c) 16
- [ ] d) 17

4) What is Malala's core belief?

- [ ] a) Children deserve the same educational rights regardless of gender.
- [ ] b) Education for girls is more important than boys.
- [ ] c) The right to education in Pakistan.
- [ ] d) To educate children to work for worldwide peace.

5) How did the gunman identify Malala?

- [ ] a) She stood up when her name was called.
- [ ] b) Her friends looked in her direction.
- [ ] c) He knew what she looked like.
- [ ] d) Her friends pointed her out.

6) Why has Malala been honoured in so many ways?

- [ ] a) She was outspoken about her beliefs in the face of death threats.
- [ ] b) She was a child when she was injured.
- [ ] c) She had strong beliefs about an important issue.
- [ ] d) She was the victim of a cruel attack.

7) What does 'rehabilitation' (line 17) mean?

- [ ] a) To undergo extensive surgery.
- [ ] b) To restore to good health.
- [ ] c) To take long-term rest.
- [ ] d) To return to your family and home.

ae © 2015 Stephen Curran

8) Why was Malala allowed to travel without protection?

- [ ] a) Her family were influential and respected in the region.
- [ ] b) Malala liked travelling on the bus with her friends.
- [ ] c) Her family did not take the Taliban's ultimatum seriously.
- [ ] d) The Pakistani army had defeated the Taliban.

9) What would Malala's family have feared most about her recovery?

- [ ] a) She would have brain damage.
- [ ] b) She would lose time at school.
- [ ] c) She may not be able to return to Pakistan.
- [ ] d) She may not want to go to school by herself again.

10) Which word best describes Malala?

- [ ] a) Apathetic
- [ ] b) Eccentric
- [ ] c) Sensible
- [ ] d) Passionate

Choose the word that has a similar meaning to the words in both sets of brackets.

11) (stumble, slip) (excursion, outing) — blunder trip falter jaunt misstep

12) (valve, spout) (knock, rap) — nozzle clout faucet tap thwack

13) (rouse, stir) (vigil, funeral) — memorial revive wake budget watch

14) (letter, message) (observe, consider) — memo watch despatch reflect note

15) (emerge, materialise) (menace, threaten) — loom scare appear surface alarm

© 2015 Stephen Curran

Choose the word that means the opposite of the word on the left.

16) **untruthful**	deceitful ☐	fictional ☐	honest ☐	altered ☐
17) **yield**	resist ☐	harvest ☐	hide ☐	produce ☐
18) **pristine**	immaculate ☐	basic ☐	spotless ☐	soiled ☐
19) **barren**	bare ☐	fertile ☐	deserted ☐	dark ☐
20) **vigilant**	slack ☐	guardian ☐	enemy ☐	attentive ☐

Complete the word on the right so that it means the same as, or nearly the same as, the word on the left.

21) **negligent**

c			e	l		s	

22) **responsible**

	c		o	u		t		b		e

23) **temperate**

m	o		e		a	t	

24) **hard-hearted**

u		f	e		l	i	n	

25) **juvenile**

y	o				f	u	

Score ☐ **Percentage** ☐ %

© 2015 Stephen Curran

Verbal Activity Test 40

Read the following passage carefully.

Poor Dog Tray

On the green banks of Shannon, when Sheelah was nigh,
No blithe Irish lad was so happy as I;
No harp like my own could so cheerily play,
And wherever I went was my poor dog Tray.

When at last I was forced from my Sheelah to part,
She said (while the sorrow was big at her heart),
"O, remember your Sheelah when far, far away;
And be kind, my dear Pat, to our poor dog Tray."

Poor dog! he was faithful and kind, to be sure,
And he constantly loved me, although I was poor;
When the sour-looking folks sent me heartless away,
I had always a friend in my poor dog Tray.

When the road was so dark, and the night was so cold,
And Pat and his dog were grown weary and old,
How snugly we slept in my old coat of gray,
And he licked me for kindness,—my poor dog Tray.

Though my wallet was scant, I remembered his case,
Nor refused my last crust to his pitiful face;
But he died at my feet on a cold winter day,
And I played a sad lament for my poor dog Tray.

Where now shall I go, poor, forsaken, and blind?
Can I find one to guide me, so faithful and kind?
To my sweet native village, so far, far away,
I can nevermore return with my poor dog Tray.

By Thomas Campbell (1777–1844).

Notes on Text:
Shannon (line 1) – a river in Ireland
Sheelah (line 1) – an Irish female name
blithe (line 2) – showing casual indifference

© 2015 Stephen Curran

Now answer the following questions.

1) What type of verse is this poem?
- [ ] a) Free verse
- [ ] b) Formal verse
- [ ] c) Blank verse
- [ ] d) Limerick

2) What is the rhyming pattern of this poem?
- [ ] a) AABB
- [ ] b) ABBA
- [ ] c) ABAB
- [ ] d) ABAC

3) What was Pat's occupation?
- [ ] a) Blacksmith
- [ ] b) Travelling musician
- [ ] c) Dog minder
- [ ] d) Beggar

4) What does the word 'lament' (line 20) mean in this poem?
- [ ] a) A mournful piece of music.
- [ ] b) An upbeat melody.
- [ ] c) A poem.
- [ ] d) A song of grief.

5) What poetic sound device is used in line 2?
- [ ] a) Alliteration
- [ ] b) Assonance
- [ ] c) Onomatopoeia
- [ ] d) Consonance

6) What does 'scant' (line 17) mean in this poem?
- [ ] a) He had lost his wallet.
- [ ] b) His clothes had worn out.
- [ ] c) He had no money.
- [ ] d) He had no bread.

ae © 2015 Stephen Curran

7) Where does Pat intend to go after Tray dies?

- [ ] a) Back to Sheelah.
- [ ] b) To another village.
- [ ] c) Back to the Shannon.
- [ ] d) Pat's future is not made clear.

8) What were Sheelah's last instructions to Pat?

- [ ] a) Do not leave me for the dog.
- [ ] b) Make sure you return and visit me.
- [ ] c) Do not forget me and take care of your dog.
- [ ] d) If you are leaving me do not come back.

9) What is the tone of this poem?

- [ ] a) Light-hearted
- [ ] b) Sentimental
- [ ] c) Contented
- [ ] d) Dreamy

10) What is the most important aspect of Tray's relationship with Pat?

- [ ] a) He is a faithful companion.
- [ ] b) He helps him earn a living.
- [ ] c) He protects him from enemies.
- [ ] d) He keeps him warm on winter nights.

Fill in the missing letters to complete the passage.

Giant pandas are black and white **11)** b _ _ _ s that mainly live in China in broadleaf and **12)** c _ n _ f e _ o _ s forests with a dense underlying layer of **13)** b _ m _ o _ . Pandas used to live in **14)** _ o w _ a _ d areas but manmade factors such as **15)** d _ v e _ o p _ e _ t , farming and forest clearing have forced them to move to **16)** m _ u n _ a i _ ranges with

© 2015 Stephen Curran

heights of 5,000 to 10,000 feet. The **17)** [_ _ j o r _ t _] of

the panda's fur is white, but there are black patches on their eyes,

18) [s _ o u _ d _ r _], ears, muzzle and legs. Giant pandas

have been **19)** [_ e p _ r _ e _] to reach the age of 35, but it is

20) [_ n _ n o _ n] what age they can reach in the wild.

Rearrange the words so that each sentence makes sense. Underline the word which does NOT fit into the sentence.

21) delayed third my four for hour journey hours one was

22) student each pack was books a a of nine given

23) it the is it as first was day very hectic was

24) printing jar several the jammed printer pages while

25) do bedroom please could chores and muddle you your up your tidy

Score [ ] **Percentage** [%]

ae © 2015 Stephen Curran

Notes

© 2015 Stephen Curran

Answers

Test 21
1) c
2) a
3) b
4) d
5) b
6) a
7) c
8) d
9) a
10) b
11) deck
12) toll
13) spring
14) pale
15) mess
16) universal
17) pleasant
18) poisonous
19) offensive
20) renowned
21) prosper
22) sensible
23) mundane
24) energy
25) current

Test 22
1) a
2) d
3) c
4) b
5) a
6) b
7) a
8) c
9) b
10) d
11) woodwind
12) reed
13) blowing
14) means
15) invented
16) century
17) descendant
18) finger
19) played
20) orchestra
21) absent
22) protect
23) unimaginative
24) unhelpful
25) considerate

Test 23
1) b
2) a
3) d
4) c
5) a
6) c
7) d
8) a
9) b
10) c
11) pester
12) sincere
13) lively
14) chartered
15) vital
16) tense
17) appear
18) ant
19) filter
20) degradation
21) cowardly
22) insufficient
23) include
24) placid
25) inattentive

Test 24
1) c
2) b
3) d
4) a
5) a
6) b
7) c
8) d
9) b
10) c
11) sowing
12) different
13) thorny
14) sprang
15) burnt
16) unable
17) shallow
18) choked
19) produce
20) yield
21) yours
22) storey
23) has
24) chose
25) puppies

Test 25
1) a
2) b
3) c
4) a
5) a
6) d
7) a
8) d
9) b
10) c
11) miserable
12) tranquil
13) abandon
14) entertaining
15) vandalise
16) volume
17) rank
18) import
19) jam
20) rock
21) keep
22) mend
23) ordinary
24) scarce
25) calm

© 2015 Stephen Curran

Answers

Test 26
1) b
2) d
3) c
4) a
5) c
6) a
7) d
8) a
9) d
10) b
11) born
12) served
13) childhood
14) most
15) followed
16) during
17) Perhaps
18) famous
19) nation's
20) disease
21) energetic
22) stylish
23) dejected
24) tattered
25) volunteer

Test 27
1) a
2) b
3) c
4) b
5) d
6) c
7) c
8) a
9) b
10) d
11) paper
12) vilify
13) Glasgow
14) intolerant
15) pay
16) yesterday
17) their
18) films
19) evening
20) are
21) accept
22) avoid
23) leave
24) secure
25) limited

Test 28
1) a
2) c
3) b
4) d
5) b
6) a
7) d
8) c
9) c
10) b
11) million
12) collectively
13) feathered
14) extinction
15) dinosaur
16) meaning
17) formally
18) impressive
19) reputation
20) carnivorous
21) remain
22) brutal
23) strong
24) blend
25) egotistical

Test 29
1) d
2) b
3) a
4) c
5) c
6) b
7) a
8) d
9) b
10) d
11) president
12) elected
13) youngest
14) expansion
15) pledged
16) space
17) assassinated
18) reality
19) remembered
20) history
21) guilty
22) gigantic
23) respectful
24) unperceptive
25) unrelated

Test 30
1) d
2) a
3) c
4) c
5) b
6) d
7) b
8) a
9) c
10) b
11) G - Olympian
12) A - twelve
13) E - overthrew
14) C - Cronus
15) I - brothers
16) D - rule
17) H - sea
18) B - Hades
19) F - three
20) J - embodied
21) hobbies
22) if
23) was
24) homework
25) cue

© 2015 Stephen Curran

Answers

Test 31
1) b
2) a
3) c
4) b
5) b
6) d
7) a
8) c
9) b
10) c
11) sociable
12) losing
13) reluctance
14) extinguish
15) transparent
16) bodybuilder
17) centaur
18) beseeched
19) atrocious
20) indigo
21) sorrow
22) biased
23) common
24) restore
25) despicable

Test 32
1) a
2) c
3) b
4) d
5) c
6) b
7) a
8) d
9) c
10) b
11) G - built
12) F - protection
13) J - introduced
14) H - England
15) D - victory
16) A - wooden
17) C - stone
18) I - size
19) B - rank
20) E - Prague
21) to
22) farmer
23) of
24) are
25) at

Test 33
1) c
2) a
3) c
4) a
5) b
6) c
7) d
8) a
9) c
10) b
11) prompt
12) contaminate
13) threatening
14) rogue
15) diminish
16) scheming
17) talented
18) foresee
19) unhappy
20) overjoyed
21) stall
22) spell
23) kid
24) duck
25) knot

Test 34
1) b
2) c
3) a
4) d
5) d
6) b
7) a
8) c
9) a
10) b
11) dreadful
12) aggressive
13) foolish
14) cheerful
15) conventional
16) moor
17) season
18) hip
19) stalk
20) lock
21) Earth
22) lever
23) exalt
24) taut
25) bolognese

Test 35
1) a
2) b
3) c
4) a
5) b
6) a
7) b
8) d
9) c
10) a
11) stable
12) fake
13) divide
14) thrifty
15) unethical
16) tender
17) rear
18) state
19) hail
20) stunt
21) infirmity
22) disloyal
23) weak
24) combine
25) bitter

© 2015 Stephen Curran

Answers

Test 36

1) b
2) c
3) a
4) d
5) b
6) a
7) c
8) b
9) d
10) c
11) B - prince
12) H - brothers
13) I - continually
14) E - disregarded
15) A - desert
16) G - mighty
17) D - pyramid
18) F - suddenly
19) C - fulfil
20) J - becoming
21) trainers
22) game
23) mouse
24) days
25) hate

Test 37

1) c
2) d
3) b
4) d
5) b
6) a
7) c
8) b
9) d
10) a
11) crisp
12) robust
13) innocent
14) industrious
15) calm
16) revolting
17) cautious
18) disdainful
19) stubborn
20) merciful
21) legend
22) crossword
23) stern
24) gangster
25) inject

Test 38

1) c
2) a
3) b
4) a
5) d
6) b
7) c
8) d
9) a
10) c
11) charity
12) education
13) volunteers
14) clock
15) different
16) collectives
17) wide
18) awareness
19) keen
20) wonderful
21) virtuous
22) dependant
23) animated
24) marvellous
25) individual

Test 39

1) c
2) d
3) b
4) a
5) b
6) a
7) b
8) c
9) a
10) d
11) trip
12) tap
13) wake
14) note
15) loom
16) honest
17) resist
18) soiled
19) fertile
20) slack
21) careless
22) accountable
23) moderate
24) unfeeling
25) youthful

Test 40

1) b
2) a
3) b
4) a
5) b
6) c
7) d
8) c
9) b
10) a
11) bears
12) coniferous
13) bamboo
14) lowland
15) development
16) mountain
17) majority
18) shoulders
19) reported
20) unknown
21) third
22) a
23) is
24) jar
25) muddle

© 2015 Stephen Curran

PROGRESS CHARTS

Test	Mark	%
21		
22		
23		
24		
25		
26		
27		
28		
29		
30		
31		
32		
33		
34		
35		
36		
37		
38		
39		
40		

CERTIFICATE OF

ACHIEVEMENT

This certifies

____

has successfully completed

11+ Verbal Activity

Year 5–7 CEM Style

TESTBOOK **2**

Overall percentage score achieved [ ] %

Comment ________________________________

____

Signed ________________________________

(teacher/parent/guardian)

Date ________________________________

SUCCESSFUL ae COMPLETION